Canon EOS 6D Mark II User Handbook

The Complete 6D Mark II Manual with Illustrations for Beginners

By

Walt Leaburn

Table of Contents

Chapter 1: Getting the Lay of the Land

Getting Comfortable with Your Lens

Attaching a lens

Here are the steps to attach a lens:

1. Make sure your camera is powered off. This is important to prevent any accidental damage or injury while attaching the lens.

2. Locate the lens release button on the bottom-right side of the lens mount on the camera body. Press and hold the lens release button.

3. Align the lens mount on the back of the lens with the lens mount on the camera body. The lens mount on the lens will have a red dot or a white square marker that should be aligned with the corresponding marker on the camera body.

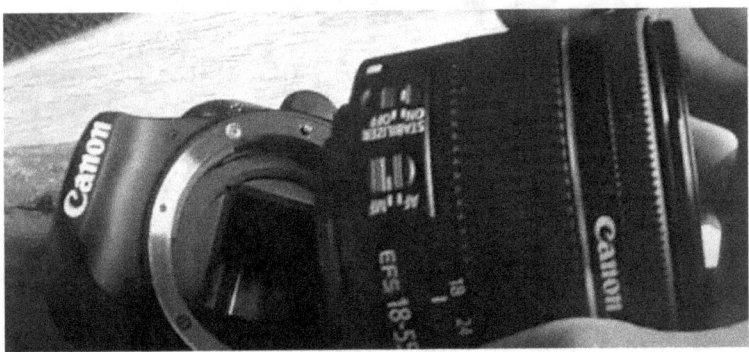

4. Once the lens is properly aligned with the camera body, gently twist the lens clockwise until it locks into place. You should hear a click sound indicating that the lens is securely attached.

5. Release the lens release button on the camera body.

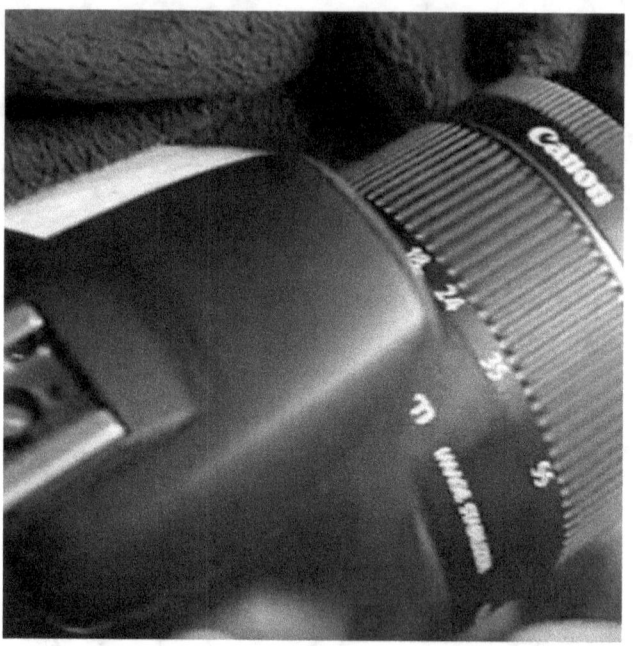

6. Power on your Canon EOS 6D Mark II camera and you're ready to use your lens!

Removing a lens

Here are the steps to remove a lens:

1. Before removing the lens, make sure the camera is turned off to avoid damaging the camera or the lens.

2. On the front of the camera body, near the lens mount, you'll find a lens release button. It is typically labeled with a white dot or symbol.

3. While keeping the camera body steady with one hand, use your other hand to press and hold the lens release button.

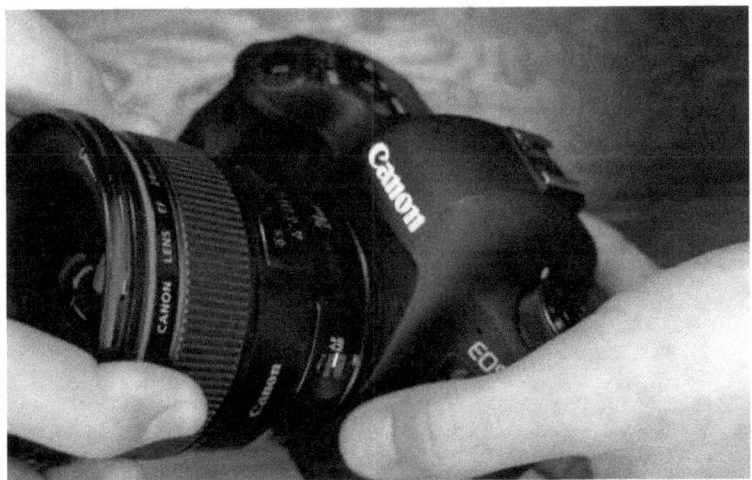

4. While holding down the lens release button, rotate the lens counterclockwise (when looking at the front of the camera) to unlock it from the lens mount.

5. Once the lens is unlocked, gently pull it straight out from the camera body. Avoid twisting or pulling forcefully, as it may damage the lens or the camera mount.

6. After removing the lens, attach the lens cap to protect the exposed lens elements from dust and scratches.

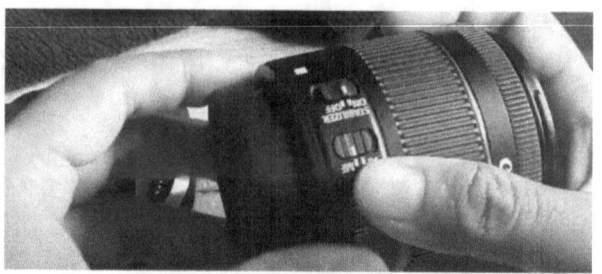

Exploring External Camera Controls

Topside Controls

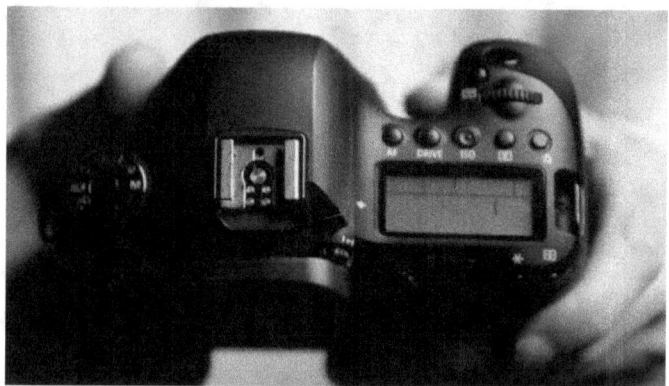

- **Mode Dial:** The mode dial is located on the top left side of the camera and allows you to select different shooting modes, including manual (M), aperture priority (Av), shutter priority (Tv), program auto exposure (P), and more. This dial gives you quick access to different shooting modes, allowing you to customize your settings based on your shooting needs.

- **Shutter Button:** The shutter button is located on the top right side of the camera and is used to take photos. A half-press of the shutter button activates autofocus, and a full press captures the image. It also has a rotating

8

dial around it, known as the Quick Control Dial, which allows you to quickly adjust settings like shutter speed, aperture, and exposure compensation.

- **Power Switch:** The power switch is located on the top left side of the camera near the mode dial and is used to turn the camera on and off.

- **Hot Shoe:** The hot shoe is located on the top of the camera and allows you to attach external accessories such as a flash, a wireless transmitter, or a microphone to enhance your photography experience.

Front View

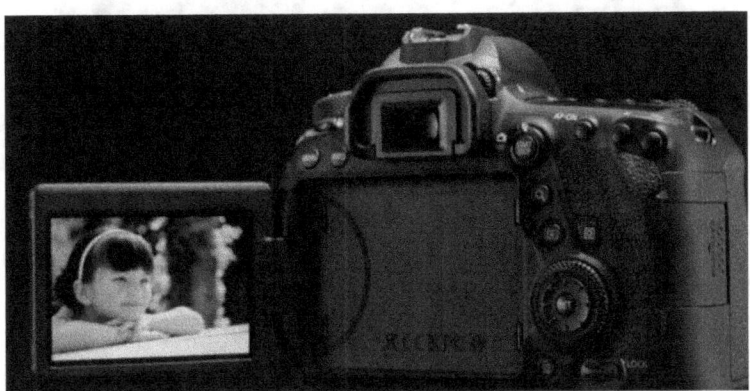

- **Lens Release Button:** The lens release button is located on the front of the camera, near the lens mount. Pressing and holding this button allows you to remove the lens from the camera.

- **Depth-of-Field Preview Button:** The depth-of-field preview button is located on the front of the camera, near the lens mount. When pressed, it stops down the aperture to the selected value, allowing you to preview the depth of field in the viewfinder or on the LCD screen.

Business End

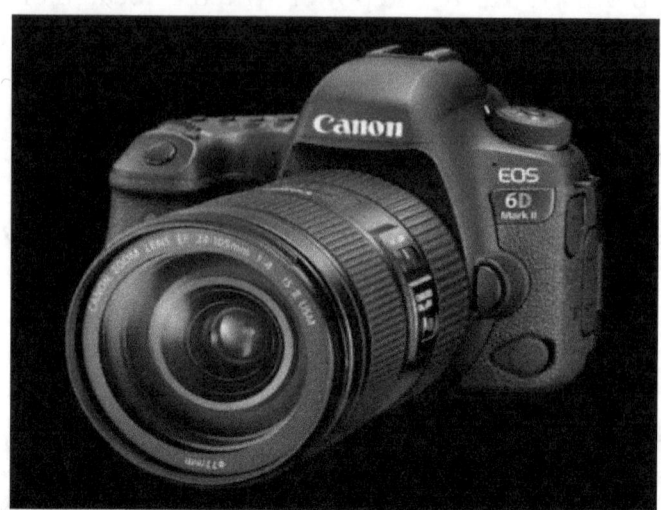

- **Lens Mount:** The lens mount is located on the front of the camera and is where you attach your compatible Canon EF or EF-S lenses. It allows you to interchange lenses to suit your shooting needs and preferences.

- **Autofocus/MF Switch:** The autofocus/manual focus (AF/MF) switch is located on the side of the lens near the lens mount. It allows you to switch between autofocus and manual focus mode, giving you control over how you want to focus on your subjects.

- **Image Stabilization Switch:** If you have a lens with image stabilization (IS) capabilities, the image stabilization switch is located on the side of the lens near the lens mount. It allows you to turn the image stabilization on or off, depending on your shooting situation.

Setting the Time and Date

You might be prompted to enter the time and date when using the Canon EOS 6D Mark II for the first time. (This data might have been entered by a third party that examined your camera before the sale on your behalf.) Just carry out these actions.

1. On the 6D Mark II's back, in the upper-left corner, press the MENU button.

2. Rotate the Main Dial until the Set-up 2 menu is highlighted (near the shutter release button on top of the camera). The wrench and the message "SET UP2" are used to identify it.

3. Turn the Quick Control Dial (QCD) so that the Date/Time entry is highlighted.

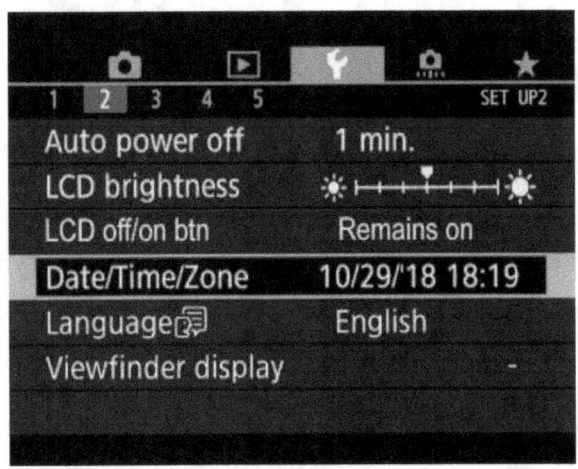

4. To access the Date/Time/Zone setting screen, press the SET button in the QCD's center. (The Main Dial and QCD locations are indicated to the left and right [respectively]

5. Rotate the QCD to choose the desired value. Use the SET button to activate the value when the month, day, year, hour, minute, or second format that you want to change is highlighted in gold. Above the value, a pair of triangles with an up/down arrow appears.

6. To change the value up or down, turn the Quick Control Dial. To confirm the figure you've entered, press the SET button.

7. Follow steps 5 and 6 again for each additional value you wish to modify. You can change the date format from the standard mm/dd/yy to yy/mm/dd or dd/mm/yy. You can choose a time zone and turn on or off Daylight Saving Time.

8. After you're done, rotate the QCD to choose OK (if you're happy with your changes) or Cancel (if you want to go back to the Set-up 2 menu screen without making any changes) by pressing the appropriate button. To confirm your selection, press SET.

9. Press the MENU button to leave after you've finished adjusting the time and date.

Choosing Shooting Mode

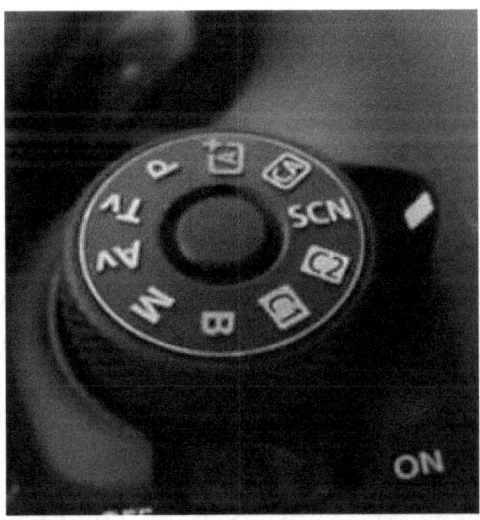

It's time to start taking pictures with your EOS 6D Mark II. The simple part is turning on the power using the OFF/ON switch located next to the Mode Dial on the top-left shoulder of the camera. If you fitted a lens, attached a new battery, and loaded a memory card before turning on the camera, you are ready to start shooting. A shooting mode, metering mode, and focus mode must all be chosen.

The Mode Dial, which is on the top-left edge of the 6D Mark II, allows you to select a shooting technique. To unlock the dial lock and turn the dial, press the button in the center. Scene Intelligent Auto, the camera's only fully automatic setting, makes almost all of your decisions (except when to press the shutter). Moreover, the Mode Dial contains an SCN position for Scene modes appropriate for common topic kinds (such as

Sports or Landscapes), as well as Creative Auto, which does allow adjusting some parameters.

The Program, Shutter-priority, Aperture-priority, Manual, and Bulb are among the five semi-automatic/manual modes (what Canon refers to as Creative Zone modes) available on the 6D Mark II. These modes let you control the exposure and settings the camera uses. Additionally, there are two custom shooting modes (also known as camera user settings) that can be used to save particular groups of camera settings. These settings can then be quickly recalled by setting the mode dial to C1 or C2.

Switch the power switch to the ON position to start your camera. The next step is to choose the shooting mode. Set the camera to Auto (the green frame on the Mode Dial) or P (Program mode) and start taking pictures if you're just getting started with digital photography. You can use these modes to create all the necessary settings for a variety of shooting scenarios.

Semi-Auto/Manual modes

The five Creativity Zone modes that can be selected from the Mode Dial are listed below. Next, I'll go into more detail on the Creative Auto and Special Scene modes.

- **P (Program):** The 6D Mark II can choose the fundamental exposure settings in this semi-automatic mode, but you can still make adjustments to your image.

- **Tv (Shutter-priority):** The temporal value (Tv) setting comes in handy when you wish to employ a certain shutter speed to freeze motion or create artistic blur effects. The 6D Mark II will choose the proper f/stop on your behalf.

- **Av (Aperture-priority):** To regulate sharpness or how much of your image is in focus, utilize Av (Aperture-priority) when selecting which lens opening to use. The 6D Mark II will choose the ideal shutter speed on your behalf. The aperture value is referred to as Av.

- **M (manual):** When you need complete control over the shutter speed and lens opening, such as when using a studio flash or another flash unit that is incompatible with the 6D Mark II's automatic flash metering, you should choose M (Manual).

- **B (bulb):** If you select B (Bulb), the shutter will stay open as long as the release button is down. Making exposures of varying lengths is advantageous (say, you want to capture some fireworks and leave the shutter open until a burst appears, then release the shutter after a few seconds when the light trails have been captured). The 6D Mark II can take automatic exposures for up to 30 seconds, although exposures longer than that can be created using the B setting.

Basic Zone Modes

Two of the Basic Zone modes that can be selected from the Mode Dial are listed below. Next, I'll go into more detail about Special Scene modes.

- **Scene Intelligent Auto/Full Auto:** The EOS 6D Mark II automatically chooses the appropriate exposure settings in this mode, shown by a green A+ icon.

- **Creative Auto:** The Creative Auto setting is much the same as the Full Auto setting, but it also lets you adjust the image's brightness and other settings. Most decisions are still made by the 6D Mark II, but you can still make a few straightforward changes by using the Creative Auto settings menu that shows when you hit the Quick Control button (located on the back of the camera to the right of the LCD monitor).

Special Scene Modes

You can choose any of the 12 Special Scene settings with the dial set to SCN. To proceed to a screen with your options listed in a vertical column, press the Q button when the screen first appears. This button is situated on the right back panel of the camera, directly above the Quick Control dial. Choose SET after selecting the desired scene mode using the up/down arrows. I'll walk you through the tiny number of tweaks that can be made while using Special Scene modes.

- **Portrait:** Use this mode to de-emphasize the backdrop, increase sharpness, and create attractive skin tones while taking a portrait of a subject who is standing near the camera.

- **Group photo:** Setting options are available to help ensure that everyone in a group photo is an intolerably sharp focus.

- **Landscape:** Use this setting for scenes that need greater sharpness and vibrant colors.

- **Sports:** Use this mode to stop moving objects in their tracks.

- **Kids:** Creates pleasing skin tones, vibrant colors, and a quick enough shutter speed to capture sharp images of rambunctious kids.

- **Panning:** By panning the camera to follow activity, you can use a slow shutter speed to produce a (relatively) crisp subject against a fuzzy background.

- **Close-up:** For taking close-up photos of a subject from no more than one foot away, this mode is useful.

- **Food:** Provides you with bold, vibrant colors to make your food appear more appealing than it probably was. Due to Instagram, taking pictures of your meal when dining out has virtually become a need.

- **Candlelight:** Preserves the warm, pleasing colors seen in candlelit objects. Even when the built-in flash is turned off, your picture will still be ruined if you have an external Speedlite connected and switched up. Switch it off!

- **Night portrait:** When you wish to use flash to spotlight a subject in the foreground while still allowing the backdrop to be correctly lit by the available light, use the night portrait mode. Having an image-stabilized (IS) lens or a tripod handy will help to lessen the impact of the camera shake. Handheld The 6D Mark II captures a night scene with four continuous photos, which it then combines to create a sharp image with minimal camera shake.

- **HDR Backlight Control:** The 6D Mark II takes three continuous shots at different exposures and combines them to produce a single image with improved detail in the highlights and shadows.

Resetting the Canon 6D Mark II

Resetting the Canon EOS 6D Mark II to its factory settings can be useful in various situations, such as troubleshooting camera issues, preparing the camera for sale or transfer, or simply starting fresh with default settings. Here are the steps to reset the Canon EOS 6D Mark II:

1. Make sure the camera is powered on and in shooting mode.

2. Press the "Menu" button located on the back of the camera, usually labeled "Menu" or represented by an icon with three horizontal lines.

3. Using the camera's arrow buttons or touch screen, navigate to the Setup menu, which is represented by a wrench icon.

4. Enter the Clear All Camera Settings option.

5. Scroll down or across the tabs until you find the "Clear All Camera Settings" option, which is usually

represented by an icon of a camera with a slash through it.

6. Select the "Clear All Camera Settings" option and press the "Set" or "OK" button. You may be prompted to confirm the reset, as it will erase all custom settings and restore the camera to its factory default settings.

7. Select "OK" or "Yes" to confirm the reset and the camera will reset to its factory default settings. This process may take a few seconds.

8. After the reset is complete, turn off the camera and then turn it back on to start using it with the default settings.

It's important to note that resetting the Canon EOS 6D Mark II will erase all custom settings, including date/time, custom functions, menu settings, and user-defined configurations. Make sure to back up any important settings or data before proceeding with the reset. Additionally, resetting the camera will not affect any saved photos on the memory card, as it only resets the camera's settings to their default values.

Chapter 2: Controlling Picture Quality and Size

Image Quality

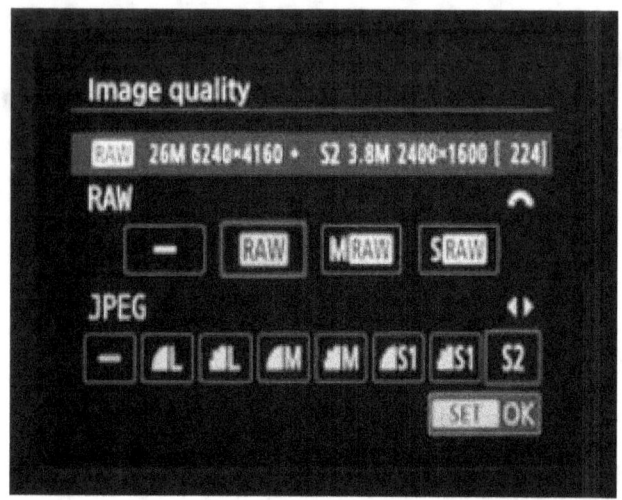

The Canon EOS 6D Mark II is a full-frame digital camera that offers a range of features and capabilities for capturing high-quality images. When it comes to image quality, the EOS 6D Mark II has several notable features that contribute to its performance.

- **Sensor and Image Processor:** The EOS 6D Mark II features a 26.2-megapixel full-frame CMOS sensor and Canon's DIGIC 7 image processor. This combination allows for high-resolution image capture with excellent image quality, dynamic range, and low noise performance, especially in low-light conditions. The sensor and image processor work together to produce detailed images with accurate colors and smooth tonal gradations.

- **ISO Performance:** The EOS 6D Mark II has a wide ISO range of 100-40000 (expandable to 50-102400), which allows for shooting in various lighting conditions. The camera's low-light performance is impressive, with relatively low noise levels even at higher ISO settings. This makes it suitable for low-light photography, such as astrophotography or indoor shooting without compromising image quality.

- **Dual Pixel CMOS AF:** The EOS 6D Mark II features Canon's Dual Pixel CMOS AF system, which provides fast and accurate autofocus performance. This autofocus system utilizes phase detection pixels on the camera's image sensor, allowing for smooth and precise autofocus, even during live view or video recording. This results in sharp images with accurate focus, contributing to overall image quality.

- **Image Formats:** The EOS 6D Mark II offers the option to capture images in both RAW and JPEG formats. RAW files contain unprocessed data captured by the sensor and provide maximum flexibility for post-processing, allowing for fine-tuning of image quality. JPEG files, on the other hand, are compressed and processed in-camera, providing smaller file sizes but with slightly less flexibility in post-processing. The camera also offers various JPEG compression options, allowing users to balance image quality with file size.

- **Lens Quality:** The quality of the lenses used with the EOS 6D Mark II can greatly impact image quality. Canon offers a wide range of high-quality lenses that are designed to work seamlessly with their full-frame cameras, including the EOS 6D Mark II. Using high-quality lenses with excellent optics, sharpness, and aberration control can help maximize the camera's image quality potential.

- **Customizable Picture Styles:** The EOS 6D Mark II provides customizable Picture Styles, which allow users to fine-tune the camera's image processing settings according to their preferences. These settings include parameters such as sharpness, contrast, saturation, and color tone, which can be adjusted to achieve desired image characteristics and optimize image quality based on the shooting situation.

Resolution (Image Size)

The Canon EOS 6D Mark II offers several resolution options for capturing images, ranging from smaller file sizes suitable for web use or quick sharing to larger file sizes for high-quality prints and professional work. The resolution settings on the Canon EOS 6D Mark II can be adjusted in the menu settings, and they are typically expressed in terms of pixels or megapixels (MP). The higher the resolution, the more pixels are used to create the image, resulting in a larger file size and potentially more detail in the final photograph.

The Canon EOS 6D Mark II offers three main resolution options:

- **Large (6240 x 4160 pixels or approximately 26.2 MP):** This is the highest resolution setting available on the Canon EOS 6D Mark II, and it is suitable for capturing images with maximum detail and clarity. This resolution is ideal for professional photographers who need to make large prints or want to capture images that can be cropped extensively without losing significant quality.

- **Medium (4160 x 2768 pixels or approximately 11.5 MP):** This resolution setting on the Canon EOS 6D Mark II is a good compromise between image quality and file size. It is suitable for general photography purposes, including printing standard-sized photos and sharing images online.

- **Small (3120 x 2080 pixels or approximately 6.5 MP):** This is the lowest resolution setting on the Canon EOS 6D Mark II, and it is ideal for web use or when file size is a consideration, such as when shooting in continuous burst mode or when storage space is limited. However, it may not be suitable for large prints or images that require extensive cropping, as it may result in a loss of detail.

It's important to note that higher-resolution images generally require more storage space and may require more processing power to edit, so it's essential to consider your specific needs when choosing a resolution setting on the Canon EOS 6D Mark II. Additionally, it's crucial to select the appropriate resolution setting based on the intended use of the final image. For example, if you plan to print large-sized photos, it's recommended to use the Large resolution setting to ensure maximum detail and sharpness.

Understanding the Image Quality Options

The Canon EOS 6D Mark II offers various image quality options that allow photographers to customize the output of their images based on their specific requirements. Image quality options determine the level of compression applied to the image file, which can affect factors such as image detail, file size, and the ability to edit and print the image. Let's take a closer look at the image quality options available on the Canon EOS 6D Mark II.

- **JPEG (Fine/Normal):** JPEG is a compressed file format that is commonly used for sharing images online or printing standard-sized photos. The Canon EOS 6D Mark II offers two JPEG quality settings: Fine and Normal. Fine compression results in less loss of image quality but larger file sizes, while Normal compression results in slightly smaller file sizes but may result in slightly reduced image quality compared to Fine.

- **RAW:** RAW is a file format that captures all the data from the camera's sensor without any compression or processing. This allows for maximum image quality and flexibility in post-processing, as RAW files retain more details, color information, and dynamic range. However, RAW files are typically larger compared to JPEG files, requiring more storage space and longer processing times. The Canon EOS 6D Mark II offers RAW image quality options such as RAW and C-RAW (Compressed

24

RAW), which provide smaller file sizes compared to standard RAW.

- **RAW + JPEG:** This option allows photographers to capture both a RAW and a JPEG version of the same image simultaneously. This can be useful for those who want to have the flexibility of RAW files for post-processing but also want to have a ready-to-share JPEG for quick sharing or printing without any additional processing.

Chapter 3: Reviewing Your Photos

Playback Menu Options

You can choose options for displaying, reviewing, transferring, and printing the images you've shot from the blue-coded Playback menus. Only three of the Playback menu items have default values, so I won't be displaying them: Picture Jump with Main Dial (10 images), Magnification (2X), and Control over HDMI (Disable).

Rotate Images

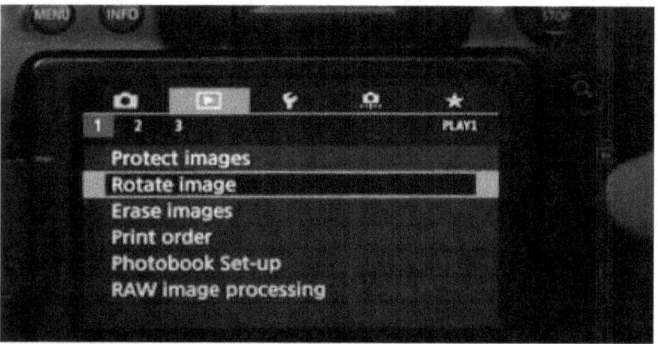

While the Auto Rotate option in the Set-up 1 menu can be used to program the EOS 6D Mark II to rotate images automatically when they are captured in a vertical orientation, you can also use this menu option to manually rotate an image while it is being played back. Choose Rotate from the Playback 1 menu, browse through the images on your memory card with the Quick Control Dial until the one you wish to rotate shows, then click SET. On the screen, the image will be 90 degrees turned.

The image will be turned 270 degrees if you press SET one more.

You have the option of selecting four options when you select this menu item: Select and Erase Pictures, Select Range, All Photos in Folder, and All Images on Card. The most current image is shown in the first selection. After rotating the Quick Control Dial to view additional images, press the SET button to designate which ones you want to delete. This marks the image for deletion. When you're done marking images, click the Trash button to bring up a box that says Erase Selected Pictures and gives you the choice between Cancel and OK. To delete the images, use the Quick Control Dial to select OK, then press the SET button. Alternatively, to return to the selection screen, select Cancel and press the SET button. To remove your selections and return to the menu, press the MENU button. Selecting a range of photographs will eliminate them all.

The All Pictures on Card option does not reformat the memory card; it just deletes all of the images on the card, excluding any that you have protected with the Protect command.

Rating

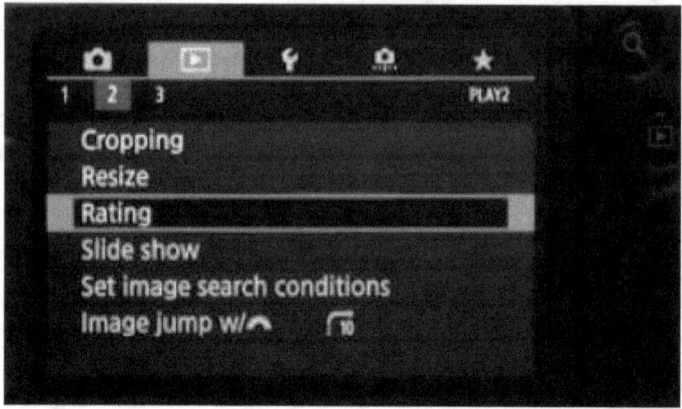

Simply press the Rating button repeatedly while the video is playing back to apply a rating to the photos or movies you've taken or use the rating system to reflect additional criteria. Or, you can use this entry to disable the rating system or assign photos one, two, three, four, or five stars. Only photographs with the specified rating can be seen using the Image Jump feature. Imagine you were taking pictures of a track meet with numerous events. Jumping events might receive a one-star rating, relays a two-star rating, throwing events a three-star rating hurdles a four-star rating, and dashes a five-star rating. The Picture Jump function would then allow you to only view specific types of photographs.

You may use the ranking system for a variety of categories if you use a little creativity. You might categorize photographs taken at a wedding of the bride, the groom, visitors, ushers, and the couple's parents. If you were taking school pictures, the first grade may fall under one classification, the second under another, and so forth. This feature has far more applications than you might imagine if you give it a little attention. Moreover, ratings can be used to choose photographs in Digital Photo Professional or to designate images for a slide show.

Simply take the following actions to use the rating menu entry:

1. Select the menu option for Rating.

2. Select from All Images on Card, All Images in Folder, Select Images, Select Range, and Select Images.

3. Using the earlier described common image selection options, choose one or more images. Press SET once an image or movie that you want to rate is visible.

4. Next, rotate the QCD to assign a rating of one to five stars or to disable a rating. A maximum of 999 photos can be rated.

5. After the rating is complete, select MENU to leave.

RAW Image Processing

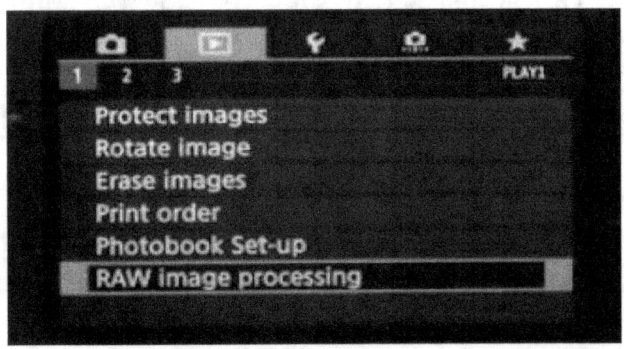

Full-size RAW images can be converted to JPEGs within the camera (but not M or S RAW files). No changes are made to the original RAW image. Only compatible RAW photos are presented to you when you choose this menu option. Just carry out these actions.

1. Select Playback from the menu. Press SET after navigating to the RAW Image Processing entry. There will only be RAW photos displayed.

2. Examine RAW pictures. To scroll through compatible images in full-frame mode, turn the Main Dial or QCD. Instead, you can view several index images by pressing the Magnify button and turning the Main Dial in the opposite direction to zoom in on a particular image.

3. Decide which image to edit. To choose a picture for processing, press SET.

4. Define the parameters. You can choose from several parameters on a screen that appears.

5. Make modifications. When a parameter is highlighted, you can adjust settings by rotating the Main Dial or QCD. Instead, you can use SET to get a screen with more precise settings. Press INFO to return the settings to the RAW image's default values, and press Magnify to enlarge the image.

6. Save JPEG files. Press SET after finding (or tapping) the Save icon, which is situated just above the Return arrow at the bottom right of the screen. Selecting Yes will create a new file; selecting Cancel will stop the

procedure. The image will be displayed in its original aspect ratio if the original was captured using live view and the aspect ratio was something other than 3:2.

Cropping

The Playback 2 menu's first item is this one. You can crop an image here if you need to. Although you don't have as much power as you would in an image editor, this can be sufficient if, for example, you need to crop an image for emailing or posting to a social media site. Only JPEG photos in the Large, Medium, S1, or S2 sizes can be cropped.

Images in every JPG format are displayed. To choose a picture for cropping, use the Main Dial or QCD. When you've decided on an image, click SET. You can then use one of these tools:

- To enlarge and minimize the green cropping frame, turn the Main Dial.

- To move the cropping frame within the image, use the multi-controller directional buttons.

- Rotate the QCD to change the cropping frame's aspect ratios from 1:1 to 3:2, 16:9, 4:3, and 4:3. You can also crop horizontally or vertically.

- Choose the "reverse" proportions to trim a horizontal image using vertical orientation instead: 2:3, 9:16, or 3:4.

- You can adjust the tilt of the image by plus or minus 10 degrees. To correct the QCD in larger 0.5-degree increments, tap the "rotate" icons displayed in the upper left corner of the screen. Press the INFO. button to rotate the QCD in 0.1-degree steps. To confirm and go, press SET.

- The cropped image will appear when you press the Q button, with the portion outside the frame deleted.

- To save your cropped image as a new file, press SET and choose OK. Your original image is preserved in its entirety.

Resize

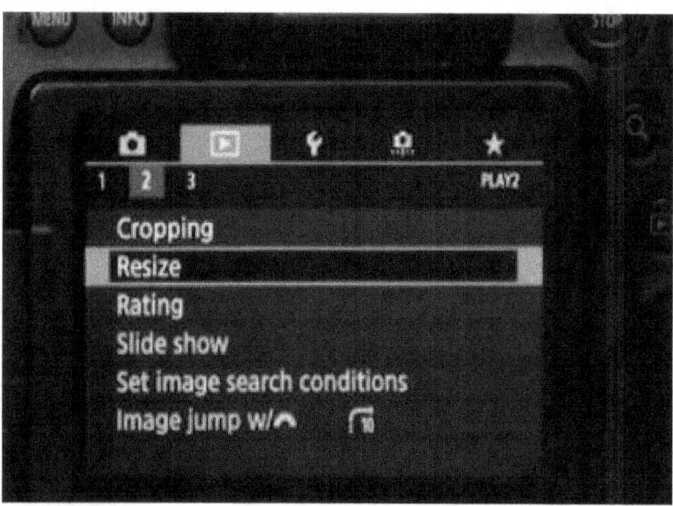

You can make a smaller version of a photograph that you've already taken using this menu entry, for example, to send via email. Just carry out these actions:

1. Select Resize. Choose Playback 2 and then this menu option.

2. To resize an image, view it. With the directional buttons or touch screen, you can scroll through the photographs that are now accessible. Only resizable photos are displayed. JPEG Big, Medium, Small 1, and Small 2 photos are among them. Any sort of RAW image cannot be scaled.

3. Decide on a picture. To choose a picture to resize, press SET. As you rotate the QCD, a pop-up menu will show up on the screen with a selection of smaller-sized photos. They are M (12MP, 4160 x 2768 pixels), S1 (6.5MP, 3210 x 2080 pixels), and S2 (2.5MP, 2400 x 1600 pixels), respectively. A JPEG Medium image cannot be saved as a JPEG Large image because you cannot enlarge an image to a size larger than its present size.

4. Resize, then save. Choose SET to save as a new file, and then OK from the pop-up menu to confirm your selection, or cancel to stop saving without saving a new version. The original image is still present.

Erase Images

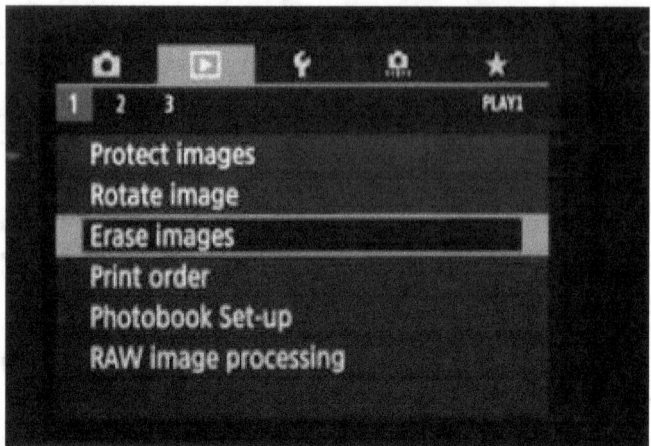

You have the option of selecting four options when you select this menu item: Select and Erase Pictures, Select Range, All Photos in Folder, and All Images on Card. The most current image is shown in the first selection. After rotating the Quick Control Dial to view additional images, press the SET button to designate which ones you want to delete. This marks the image for deletion. When you're done marking images, click the Trash button to bring up a box that says Erase Selected Pictures and gives you the choice between Cancel and OK. To delete the images, use the Quick Control Dial to select OK, then press the SET button. Alternatively, to return to the selection screen, select Cancel and press the SET button. To remove your selections and return to the menu, press the MENU button. Selecting a range of photographs will eliminate them all.

The All Pictures on Card option does not reformat the memory card; it just deletes all of the images on the card, excluding any that you have protected with the Protect command.

Protect Images

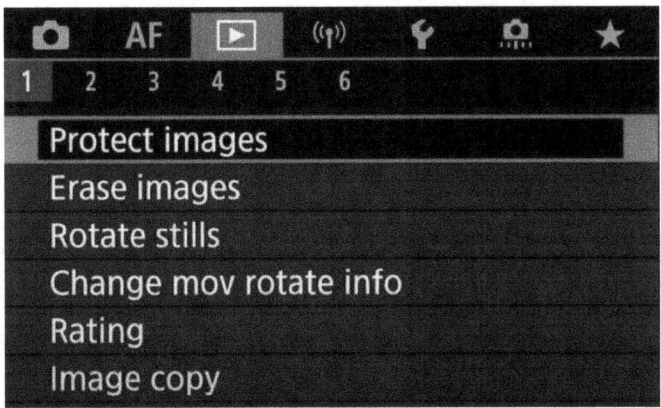

The Playback 1 menu's first of six entries is this one. You can mark an image as protected if you don't want it to be unintentionally deleted using the Erase menu or the Erase button. One or more photos can be secured in one of two methods.

- **Q button:** The Q button is arguably among the quickest methods for securing a single image. Use the Q button to view a photo in playback mode. A Quick Control screen with options for playback functions in the left column appears. When highlighted, the Protect button at the top of the screen gives you the option to either Disable or Enable marking an image as protected. You may secure the image from this screen with a few taps on the touch screen or by using the standard controls. To protect multiple pictures, click DETAILS. Choose Range, All Pictures on Card, and Unprotect All Photos on Card are your options.

- **Playback menu:** You should utilize this menu option, which provides more options, to protect multiple photos. When you select Preserve Pictures, a screen with six options appears:

- **Select images:** Choose a single image and then hit SET.

- **Select a range:** Press SET to mark the first image as protected, then scroll or go to the last image and click SET once more.

- **Every photo in the folder:** A list of accessible folders will be displayed. Choose one, then hit SET.

- **Unprotect All Images in Folder:** Use this to unmark/unprotect images in a folder of your choice.

- **All Images on Card:** Protects all images on your memory card.

- **Unprotect All Images on Card:** Removes protection from all the images on your card

When the photographs are presented on the screen and you pick Select Images, you can view and select specific images while also enabling protection by pressing the SET button. While viewing that image later while it is still on the protection screen, a key icon will be shown at the upper edge of the information display. Repeat the procedure to remove protection. With the QCD, you can navigate through the other photos on your memory card and protect or unprotect them in the same way. When the card is reformatted, image protection will not prevent your photographs from being deleted.

Chapter 4: Getting Creative with Exposure and Lighting

Introducing the Exposure Trio: Aperture, Shutter Speed, and ISO

The Exposure Trio, consisting of Aperture, Shutter Speed, and ISO, are the three fundamental components of photography that work together to control the exposure and creative outcome of a photograph. Understanding how these three elements interact with each other is crucial for achieving desired results in photography.

- **Aperture:** Aperture refers to the size of the lens diaphragm opening in a camera, which determines the amount of light that enters the camera through the lens. It is typically expressed as an f-stop value, such as f/1.8, f/5.6, f/11, etc. A smaller f-stop value (e.g., f/1.8) indicates a larger aperture opening, allowing more light to enter, while a larger f-stop value (e.g., f/16) indicates a smaller aperture opening, allowing less light to enter. Aperture also affects the depth of field in a photograph, which determines the amount of foreground and background blur.

- **Shutter Speed:** Shutter speed refers to the duration for which the camera's shutter remains open, allowing light to reach the camera sensor. It is typically measured in fractions of a second, such as 1/500, 1/60, 1/15, etc. A faster shutter speed (e.g., 1/1000) allows less light to enter, and it freezes motion in the photograph, while a

38

slower shutter speed (e.g., 1/15) allows more light to enter, and it may introduce motion blur in the photograph.

- **ISO:** ISO refers to the sensitivity of the camera's image sensor to light. It is typically represented as an ISO value, such as ISO 100, ISO 400, ISO 1600, etc. A lower ISO value (e.g., ISO 100) indicates lower sensitivity to light, suitable for bright conditions, while a higher ISO value (e.g., ISO 1600) indicates a higher sensitivity to light, suitable for low-light conditions. However, higher ISO values may introduce digital noise or graininess in the photograph.

Choosing an Exposure Metering Mode

The Canon EOS 6D Mark II is a popular digital SLR camera that offers various metering modes for different shooting situations. The metering mode determines how the camera measures the light in the scene to calculate the correct exposure settings. Here are the metering modes available on the Canon EOS 6D Mark II and when you might want to use them:

- **Evaluative Metering:** This is the default metering mode on the EOS 6D Mark II. It uses a complex system that divides the scene into multiple zones and evaluates the light in each zone to calculate the overall exposure. It's ideal for general shooting situations when you want the camera to consider the entire scene for accurate exposure.

- **Partial Metering:** In this mode, the camera meters the central part of the scene, usually around 6-10% of the frame. It's useful when you have a subject that is backlit or in a situation where the background is much brighter than the subject. It can help you achieve a more accurate exposure to the subject while preserving the details in the brighter areas.

- **Spot Metering:** This mode meters a very small area, usually around 2-3% of the frame, centered on the active AF point. It's useful when you want to meter for a specific area or subject in the scene, such as a person's face or a small subject against a bright or dark background.

- **Center-Weighted Average Metering:** This mode gives more importance to the light in the center of the frame and less weight to the surrounding areas. It's useful when you want to give priority to the subject in the center of the frame and have less concern for the exposure of the surrounding areas.

Applying Exposure Compensation

Exposure compensation is a useful feature that allows you to override the camera's automatic exposure settings to make your photos brighter or darker as needed. You can use it to adjust the exposure when the camera's metering system may not accurately reflect your desired exposure, such as in high-contrast scenes or when you intentionally want to create a specific mood or effect in your photos. Here's how you can apply exposure compensation on the Canon EOS 6D Mark II:

- Make sure your camera is in a mode that allows exposure compensation, such as Program (P), Shutter Priority (Tv), Aperture Priority (Av), or Manual (M). These modes give you control over exposure settings.

- Press the exposure compensation button, which is usually labeled with a "+/-" symbol and located near the shutter button or on the back of the camera. On the EOS 6D Mark II, the exposure compensation button is typically located on the top right of the camera, marked with a "+/-" symbol.

- Use the main dial, which is usually located near the shutter button, to adjust the exposure compensation value. Turning the dial to the right (clockwise) will make your photo brighter (increasing exposure compensation) while turning it to the left (counterclockwise) will make it darker (decreasing exposure compensation). The exact range of exposure compensation values may vary depending on your camera's settings, but typically it ranges from -3 to +3 stops in 1/3-stop increments.

- As you adjust the exposure compensation value, you will see the changes reflected in the camera's viewfinder or on the rear LCD screen. This allows you to preview the exposure adjustments in real time.

- Once you have set the desired exposure compensation value, half-press the shutter button to lock in the exposure settings, or simply release the exposure compensation button to apply the adjustment.

- Remember to reset the exposure compensation value back to zero (0) when you're done using it, as it remains active until you manually reset it. You can do this by either setting the exposure compensation value back to 0 using the exposure compensation button and main dial, or by simply turning off the camera.

Note: Exposure compensation is typically not available in fully automatic modes like Auto (A+) or Scene modes, as the camera's exposure settings are determined automatically in those modes. Be sure to use a mode that allows manual control, as mentioned in step 1, to use exposure compensation on the Canon EOS 6D Mark II.

Tonal Range

Tonal range is the range of tones that can be caught in a photograph or displayed in an image, from the darkest to the brightest. It is frequently linked to the idea of dynamic range, which is the range between an image's darkest and brightest areas where detail can be preserved or exhibited without loss.

The tonal range is significant in photography because it has a direct impact on the amount of detail and contrasts in an image. A photograph with a larger tonal range will have more clarity and contrast in the shadows, mid-tones, and highlights, making it more aesthetically appealing and lively.

42

The Canon EOS 6D Mark II and other contemporary digital cameras commonly feature a wide tonal range and are able to capture a variety of tones. However, additional elements like the caliber of the camera's sensor, the image format (such as JPEG or RAW), and the exposure settings applied during capture also affect the tonal range that may be properly captured.

Photographers can adjust an image's tonal range in post-processing by using programs like Adobe Lightroom or Photoshop. To get the desired appearance and feel for the photograph, this may entail altering the brightness and contrast, pulling out features from shadows or highlights, and making other tonal modifications.

Your ability to capture and alter tone range in your photographs can have a significant impact on their overall quality and visual impact, enabling you to take photos that are both visually appealing and expressive.

Chapter 5: Working on Your Picture Files

Sending Pictures to the Computer

To send pictures from your Canon EOS 6D Mark II to your computer, you can use one of the following methods:

- **USB Cable:** Connect your camera to your computer using a USB cable. The Canon EOS 6D Mark II comes with a USB cable that allows you to connect the camera to your computer. Simply plug one end of the USB cable into the camera's USB port, which is located on the side of the camera, and the other end into a USB port on your computer. Turn on your camera and set it to the appropriate mode (e.g., playback mode). Your computer should recognize the camera as a connected device, and you can then transfer the pictures from the camera to your computer using a file transfer utility or by simply dragging and dropping the image files to a location on your computer.

- **Memory Card Reader:** If your computer has a built-in memory card reader or if you have an external memory card reader, you can remove the memory card from your Canon EOS 6D Mark II and insert it into the memory card reader. Once inserted, your computer should recognize the memory card as a removable storage device, and you can then transfer the pictures from the memory card to your computer using a file transfer utility or by dragging and dropping the image files to a location on your computer.

- **Wi-Fi/NFC:** The Canon EOS 6D Mark II also has built-in Wi-Fi and NFC (Near Field Communication) capabilities, which allow you to transfer pictures wirelessly to your computer or other devices. You can connect your camera to your computer over Wi-Fi and use Canon's EOS Utility software, which can be downloaded from Canon's website, to transfer images wirelessly. Alternatively, you can also use the Canon Camera Connect app, which is available for download on your smartphone or tablet, to transfer images from your camera to your mobile device and then transfer them to your computer using other methods like email or cloud storage.

Connecting the camera and computer

To connect your Canon EOS 6D Mark II camera to your computer, you can use a USB cable. Here's how:

1. Power off your camera and your computer.

2. Locate the USB port on your Canon EOS 6D Mark II camera. The USB port is typically located on the side of the camera body.

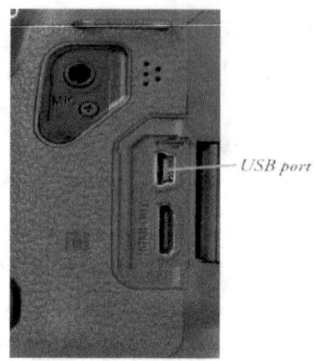

USB port

3. Connect one end of the USB cable to the USB port on your Canon EOS 6D Mark II camera.

4. Locate an available USB port on your computer. USB ports are usually found on the side or back of the computer.

5. Connect the other end of the USB cable to the USB port on your computer.

6. Power on your camera and your computer.

7. Set your Canon EOS 6D Mark II camera to the appropriate mode for image transfer. This can typically be done by turning the camera's mode dial to the playback mode, which is usually indicated by a "play" icon.

8. Your computer should now recognize the camera as a connected device. You may see a notification on your computer indicating that a new device has been detected.

9. Depending on your operating system, you may need to install drivers or software for your Canon EOS 6D Mark II camera. If prompted, follow the on-screen instructions to install any necessary drivers or software.

10. Once your camera is recognized by your computer, you can transfer images from your camera to your computer using a file transfer utility or by dragging and dropping the image files to a location on your computer.

Starting the transfer process

Once your Canon EOS 6D Mark II camera is connected to your computer via USB, and your computer has recognized the camera as a connected device, you can start the image transfer process. Here's how:

- Make sure your camera is powered on and set to the appropriate mode for image transfer, typically the playback mode, which is usually indicated by a "play" icon on the mode dial.

- On your computer, open a file transfer utility or file explorer window to navigate to the location where you want to transfer the images from your camera.

- In the file transfer utility or file explorer window, locate the connected camera device or memory card. It may be listed as a removable storage device or as the camera's model name.

- Double-click on the connected camera device or memory card to open it and access the image files stored on your Canon EOS 6D Mark II camera.

- Select the image files you want to transfer to your computer. You can usually do this by clicking and dragging over the image files to highlight them, or by using the Ctrl or Command key to select multiple files.

- Drag and drop the selected image files from the connected camera device or memory card to the destination folder on your computer. Alternatively, you can right-click on the selected image files and choose "Copy" or "Cut" from the context menu, and then right-click in the destination folder and choose "Paste" to transfer the files.

- Wait for the image files to transfer from your Canon EOS 6D Mark II camera to your computer. The transfer speed will depend on the size and number of files being transferred, as well as the performance of your computer and USB connection.

- Once the image files have been transferred, you can disconnect your Canon EOS 6D Mark II camera from your computer by safely ejecting the camera device or memory card. This can usually be done by right-clicking on the camera device or memory card in the file explorer window and choosing "Eject" or "Safely Remove".

- You can now access and view the transferred images on your computer in the destination folder where you transferred them.

Downloading and Organizing Photos with the Canon Software

Canon provides a software suite called "Canon EOS Utility" that you can use to download and organize photos from your Canon EOS 6D Mark II camera. Here's how you can use the Canon EOS Utility to download and organize your photos:

- Install Canon EOS Utility: If you haven't already installed the Canon EOS Utility software on your computer, you can download it from Canon's official website (https://www.usa.canon.com/support). Follow the on-screen instructions to install the software on your computer.

- Connect your Canon EOS 6D Mark II camera to your computer using a USB cable as described in the previous response.

- Power on your camera and set it to the appropriate mode for image transfer, typically the playback mode.

- Launch Canon EOS Utility on your computer. You should see your camera detected by the software.

- In Canon EOS Utility, you can choose to download all the images from your camera or select specific images to download. You can also choose the destination folder where you want the images to be downloaded.

- Once the images are downloaded, you can use Canon EOS Utility to organize and manage your photos. You can add metadata, such as keywords, ratings, and

49

copyright information to your photos. You can also create folders, rename files, and perform basic image editing tasks.

- Canon EOS Utility also provides options for remote shooting, where you can control your Canon EOS 6D Mark II camera from your computer and capture images remotely.

- Once you have organized your photos using Canon EOS Utility, you can export or save them to your desired location on your computer for further use, such as viewing, editing, or sharing.

Downloading with Canon EOS Utility Software

Here's a step-by-step guide on how to download photos from your Canon EOS 6D Mark II camera using Canon EOS Utility software:

1. Connect your Canon EOS 6D Mark II camera to your computer using a USB cable as described in the previous responses. Make sure your camera is powered on and set to the appropriate mode for image transfer, typically the playback mode.

2. Launch Canon EOS Utility on your computer. You can usually find it in the list of installed programs or the Applications folder, depending on your operating system.

3. Once Canon EOS Utility is launched, it should automatically detect your connected Canon EOS 6D

Mark II camera and display the camera's information on the screen.

4. In Canon EOS Utility, you can choose to download all the images from your camera or select specific images to download. To download all images, click on the "Download images" button. To select specific images, click on the "Remote Shooting/Viewing" button, and then click on the "Remote Shooting" tab. From there, you can remotely control your camera and select images to download.

5. Choose the destination folder where you want the images to be downloaded. You can do this by clicking on the "Browse" button and navigating to the desired folder on your computer.

6. Optionally, you can specify additional settings such as file format, file naming convention, and other metadata options.

7. Click on the "Download" or "Start Download" buttons to begin the download process. Canon EOS Utility will transfer the selected images from your Canon EOS 6D Mark II camera to the specified destination folder on your computer.

8. Once the download is complete, you can close Canon EOS Utility and access the downloaded images in the destination folder on your computer.

Browsing images with the main dial

The main dial on the Canon EOS 6D Mark II camera can be used to browse through images during playback mode. Here's how you can use the main dial to browse images:

- Power on your Canon EOS 6D Mark II camera and set it to playback mode. You can do this by pressing the "Play" button (marked with a triangle icon) on the back of the camera.

- Use the main dial, which is usually located near the shutter button on the top of the camera, to scroll through the images. Turning the main dial clockwise will display the next image while turning it counterclockwise will display the previous image.

- You can also use the main dial to zoom in on an image during playback mode. To do this, press the "Magnify" button (marked with a magnifying glass icon) on the back of the camera, and then turn the main dial to zoom in or out of the image.

- If you have multiple images displayed on the screen as thumbnails, you can use the main dial to navigate between the thumbnails. Turning the main dial clockwise will move the selection box to the right while turning it counterclockwise will move the selection box to the left.

- In addition to browsing through images, the main dial can also be used for other functions during playback mode, such as changing the display mode, rotating images, and deleting images. You can refer to your Canon EOS 6D Mark II camera's user manual for more information on these functions and how to use the main dial for them.

Chapter 6: Using Live View

Shooting Menu Options

Here are the shooting menu options available on the Canon EOS 6D Mark II camera:

- **Image Quality:** This option allows you to set the image quality for your photos. You can choose from various options, such as JPEG and RAW

- **image formats:** JPEG is a compressed image format that is smaller in file size and suitable for sharing online or printing smaller-sized photos. RAW is an uncompressed image format that retains more image data and provides greater flexibility for post-processing but produces larger file sizes. C-RAW is a smaller RAW format that combines the advantages of RAW and JPEG, providing smaller file sizes while still retaining the Flexibility of RAW. RAW + JPEG allows you to save both a RAW and a JPEG image of the same shot simultaneously.

- **Image Size:** This option allows you to set the image size for your photos, which determines the resolution in pixels: You can choose from various image size options, such as Large, Medium, or Small, depending on your needs. Larger image sizes provide higher resolution and more details but may result in larger file sizes, while smaller image sizes provide lower resolution but smaller file sizes.

- **White Balance:** This option allows you to set the white balance for your photos, which determines the color temperature and color balance of the image. White balance is important for achieving accurate color reproduction in different lighting conditions. You can choose from various white balance presets, such as Daylight, Cloudy, Tungsten, Fluorescent, or Custom. Custom white balance allows you to manually set the white balance using a neutral white or gray reference, such as a white card or a gray card, for accurate color reproduction in specific lighting conditions.

- **Auto Lighting Optimizer:** This option adjusts the brightness and contrast of your photos to optimize the image quality in high-contrast situations. You can choose from various Auto Lighting Optimizer settings, such as Off, Low, Standard, or High, depending on the scene you are shooting. This feature can help to recover shadow and highlight details in challenging lighting conditions, such as backlit scenes or scenes with harsh contrast.

- **High ISO Speed Noise Reduction:** This option reduces the noise in photos taken at high ISO settings, which can occur in low-light conditions. You can choose from various High ISO Speed Noise Reduction settings, such as Off, Low, Standard, or High, depending on the level of noise reduction you desire. Higher ISO settings are typically used in low-light situations to capture brighter images, but can result in increased noise, which can degrade image quality. This feature can help to reduce noise and preserve image details when shooting at high ISO settings.

- **Picture Style:** This option allows you to set the Picture Style for your photos, which determines the overall look and feel of the image, including the color saturation, sharpness, contrast, and tone. You can choose from various Picture Style presets, such as Standard, Portrait, Landscape, Neutral, Faithful, Monochrome, or User-Defined, or you can create your own custom Picture Style. Picture Styles are similar to the "film modes" of traditional film cameras, and allow you to apply different image processing settings to achieve a specific look or mood in your photos.

- **Auto Exposure Bracketing (AEB):** This option allows you to set the exposure bracketing for your photos, which captures multiple shots with different exposure settings to ensure that you capture the correct exposure. You can choose from various AEB settings, such as the number of shots, the exposure increment, and the exposure sequence. Exposure bracketing can be useful in situations where the lighting conditions are changing rapidly, or when you want to capture multiple exposures for HDR (High Dynamic Range) or blending purposes in post-processing.

- **Custom Controls:** This option allows you to customize the functions of various buttons and dials on your camera, allowing you to quickly access commonly used settings or functions during shooting. You can assign different functions to buttons or dials, such as ISO,

White Balance, Metering Mode, AF Point selection, or Depth of Field Preview.

- **AF (Autofocus) Menu:** This option allows you to configure the autofocus settings on your camera, including the AF mode, AF point selection, AF operation, and AF assist beam. You can choose from various AF settings, such as One-Shot AF, AI Servo AF, AI Focus AF, Single-point AF, Zone AF, or Automatic AF point selection, depending on your shooting requirements.

AF Method

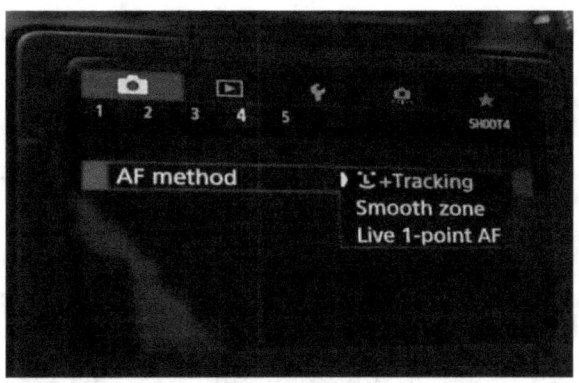

The autofocus mode, Face Detection+Tracking, Smooth Zone, and Live 1-Point AF, which are AF methods that include facial recognition, manual focus zone selection, or single focus region selection, can all be chosen from this menu. For my recommendations on picking an AF approach and other autofocus choices, see "Focusing in Live View."

Touch Shutter

When Touch Shutter is turned on in live view modes, you can tap an object on the screen to start focusing on it and shoot a photo. As soon as the focus point turns green, the picture is taken. The area you touched will turn orange and the photo won't be taken if the 6D Mark II is unable to focus. To try again, tap the subject once more. By clicking the Touch Shutter icon in the bottom-left corner of the touch screen, you can enable or disable the Touch Shutter if you don't want to use this menu option. Press the INFO button repeatedly until you see the icon if you don't see it on the screen.

Metering Timer

The EOS 6D Mark II's metering system has an option that lets you control how long it will operate before turning off. After the timer shuts off, tap the shutter release to restart it. When operating in the Basic Zone mode, this option is not accessible.

Grid Display

When enabled, this setting overlays one of three distinct grids on the screen to assist you in aligning vertical and horizontal lines and helping you compose your image. You can select a grid with three by three cells that follow the "rule of thirds" or one with four rows and six boxes, which gives you more choice over where the images are placed in your frame. A third grid also has a 3 3 design, but it also has diagonal lines.

Exposure Simulation

You can select this option to determine whether the screen displays a bright image (dependent on the LCD Brightness setting you've specified in the Set-up 2 menu) that may be easier to view in bright ambient lighting conditions, or whether the live view image mimics the exposure level of the final image.

You have the following options:

- Enable: Based on the current exposure settings, including any exposure compensation you've defined, the brightness level of the live view image on the screen matches the brightness level of the actual image. When you wish to be able to observe the results of your exposure settings in live view roughly (but not precisely), choose this option.

- In the DOF Preview When you press the depth-of-field preview button, the live view image's brightness will be changed to simulate your exposure settings. When you occasionally want to check exposure during a shooting session, this is your best option. I frequently use this setting since I can compose with a large, bright screen and still stop down to the intended aperture and observe the results.

- Disable: The 6D Mark II displays the live view image at its default brightness regardless of any exposure adjustment or settings. This setting is advantageous when used outdoors in direct sunshine because any exposure simulation (dimmed LCD) will be challenging to understand in bright conditions.

Silent LV Shooting

Canon provides you with two options for muting the shutter noise of the 6D Mark II, albeit it is not possible to totally do so. Silent live view shooting is quite quiet since Live View mode stops the obtrusive mirror-flap motion. When utilizing an electronic flash, silent photography is not possible, and if you use Mode 1 or Mode 2 with a lens that is attached to an extension tube or if you are using a Canon tilt-shift (TS-E) lens other than the TS-E17mm f/4L or TSE-E24mm f/3.5L II lenses, your exposures will be inconsistent.

At the time of writing this book, canon has not stated if the new TS-E 50mm F2.8L Macro, TS-E 90mm F2.8L Macro, and TS-E 135mm F4L Macro lenses are compatible with Quiet LV shooting.

You have the following choices:

- **Mode 1:** This option enables continuous shooting but creates a lower firing sound level in Live View mode.

- **Mode 2:** Although it technically isn't any quieter, this mode distinguishes between the ker and clunk sounds. When you fully press the shutter release, the camera takes the photo and emits a small click. After that, the camera operation is suspended as long as you continue to press the shutter button. You can choose to wait a little while before releasing the button completely or halfway, which results in a second quiet click. It's marginally less obtrusive than Mode 1, and if there's enough background noise, it's the closest a digital SLR will ever come to silent photography. Although it can be selected, continuous shooting is not available in this mode. There will only be one exposed image. If you're using a remote control, the camera ignores this setting and switches to Mode 1 by default.

- **Disable:** Disables quiet firing, albeit the resulting noises are similar to Mode 1 in terms of volume.

Shooting in Live View

After making your menu modifications and turning on live view for later use, you may choose between snapping images normally through the viewfinder of the 6D Mark II or in live view. When you're ready to start live view, make sure the Live View/Movie switch is positioned so that it looks like a camera icon, then push the Start/Stop button on the camera's back. The sensor image will show up on the Display as the mirror flips up. By pressing the INFO button, the display may be switched between being blank (aside from the image), displaying basic shooting data, all settings, and adding a live histogram. It should be noted that tapping the icons encircled by a box will modify the value of that icon.

Changing the Live View Display

Not all of the shown icons appear at once. In fact, as you cycle through the panels using the INFO button, you may somewhat control what information is displayed during live view (and video) shooting. You may learn how to alter your live view and movie displays in this section. An overview first.

- **Four potential displays:** When you push the INFO button, the screens alternate between a minimum of one and a maximum of four separate displays. In other words, if Screen 1 is displayed, pushing the button advances you to Screens 2, 3, and 4 before returning to Screen 1.

- **Turn on or off screens:** By checking the box next to a screen's label, you can specify which of the four displays is active. If all of the screens are unmarked, Screen 1 will automatically be enabled, and there must be at least one active screen.

- **Information for each screen:** Each panel offers a choice of five different forms of information, including a histogram, an electronic level, on-screen buttons, basic and detailed shooting information. Next, I'll walk you through setting up these screens.

Simply follow these procedures to enable/disable and specify up to four screens:

1. **Switch to live view:** The INFO Button LV Display Options menu entry cannot be accessed unless Live View mode is selected. Hit the Start/Stop and MENU buttons, then select Set-up 4 from the menu by selecting the second option from the bottom. Choose SET.

2. **Choose switch settings:** On the following screen, select Live View Info Switch Setting and then press SET.

3. **Turn on/off screens 1-4:** Choose any or all of the numbers at the right and press SET to add or remove a

check mark from the box next to that number in order to use the default screen settings. All four cannot be deselected; at least one screen must be active.

4. **Make each screen your own:** If you don't want to use the default values, you can add or remove information types from each screen. Press the INFO button after highlighting the screen number.

5. Highlight each of the five informational options to enable or disable it, then press SET to add or remove a checkmark. These five items can be turned on or off (leaving a blank screen in their place), from top to bottom:

- **Basic Shooting Informations:** displays data such as the shooting mode, the number of remaining exposures, the battery level, the shutter speed, the aperture, the exposure, and the ISO.

- **Display Shooting Information:** Adds columns containing autofocus, metering mode, image quality, white balance, and other information to the left and right of the screen.

- **On-Screen buttons:** Touch-sensitive buttons are added to the screen so users can reach the Quick Control Screen and Zoom level.

- **Histogram Display:** Displaying a brightness or RGB histogram in the top-right corner of the screen is known as histogram display. From the screen you saw in Step 2, you can select the kind of histogram to display and whether it appears in large or small size.

- **Electronic Level:** Whether working with Live 1-Point AF or Smooth Zone AF, the electronic level will show up; when using Face Detection+Tracking, it is disabled.

- **Confirm and Exit:** After making your selections, select or tap the OK button at the bottom of each screen to finish.

By choosing Reset from the first screen, you may restore the default settings for the Live View Button Display Settings. These are those values:

- **Screen 1:** Basic Shooting Info, On-Screen Buttons

- **Screen 2:** Basic Shooting Info, Detailed Shooting Info, On-Screen Buttons

- **Screen 3:** Basic Shooting Info, Detailed Shooting Info, On-Screen Buttons, Histogram, Electronic Level

- **Screen 4:** No information

Quick Control

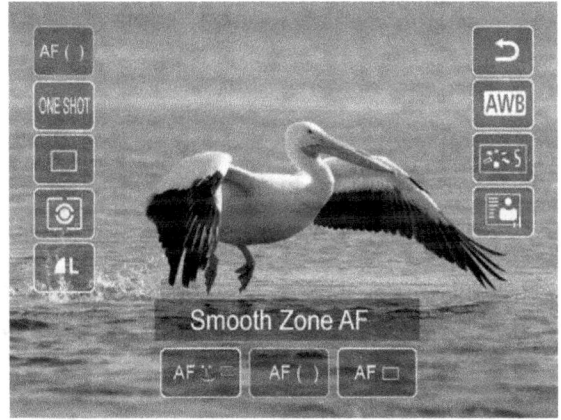

In Live View, you can get to the Quick Control screen. When On-Screen Buttons are enabled and you are in the Creative Zone mode, just press the Q button or tap the Q icon at the top right of the touch screen (as described above). The values displayed in the left and right columns can then be changed. This consists of the Auto Lighting Optimizer settings, Drive mode, White Balance, Picture Style, AF mode, and Creativity filters. Depending on the Basic Zone mode you are using, you can alter the AF mode, Drive mode, and a number of other options.

Focusing in Live View

To use the presently selected live view autofocus mode, press the shutter button halfway. You have the option of using Live 1-Point AF, Smooth Zone AF, or Face Detection+Tracking as your AF mode. They control the process by which the 6D Mark II chooses an area to concentrate on. Also, you can choose between One-Shot and Servo AF operations, which govern when the focus is locked. If you prefer to set the focus manually, that option is also accessible.

When using live view, you can switch the focus mode by pressing the Q button or tapping the Q icon on the touch screen to access the Quick Control menu. From there, you can choose the AF Method and AF operation options, While live view is on, AF Method is now accessible from the Shooting 5 menu. I'll go over each of these in turn.

Selecting an AF Method

There are three AF techniques, as I previously stated: Facial Detection+Tracking, Smooth Zone AF, or Live 1-Point AF. The latter two, which take the place of FlexiZone-Multi and FlexiZone-Single in early Canon Rebel models, are distinct from the former two. The next part gives an overview of the three current approaches.

Mode for Face Detection and Tracking

In order to focus on a human face, the 6D Mark II will scan the frame for one. It should be noted that utilizing this mode prevents you from viewing your image in magnified form. These procedures should be followed to autofocus utilizing the Face Detection+Tracking mode:

1. Set the autofocus on the lens. Ensure that the lens' focus switch is set to autofocus (AF).

2. Switch on live view. Choose "Start/Stop" on your keyboard. Choose Face Detection+Tracking from the live view Shooting 5 menu or the Quick Control menu.

3. Facial recognition, third. An image's face will have a frame around it. The frame will be green if there is only one face identified; if there are several faces, the frame will be white with left/right triangles bordering it. Use the directional controls to shift the frame to the face you wish to utilize as the focus in that situation. If no faces are found, the AF focus frame is shown and the focus is locked to the middle.

4. Focus: When the Face Detection frame is in place, halfway press the shutter button to focus the camera on the subject's face. The beeper will chime if it is turned on and the AF frame will turn green when focus is locked in. The AF frame will become orange if focus cannot be obtained.

5. In order to take the picture, press and hold the shutter release. For the photo to be taken, fully depress the shutter release.

Focus Operation

Two of the three focus operation modes for still photography—One-Shot and Servo—are available in Live view (the equivalent of AI Servo). When shooting with live view, AI AF, which automatically alternates between One-Shot and AI Servo in still mode, is not an option. To help you remember how various modes operate, below is a summary.

Movie Shooting Menus

Videography is pretty straightforward, but there are a few additional considerations you should make before you begin. You will learn everything you need to know in this section before you start taking videos seriously. The Shooting menu movie screens become available when the LV selection switch is turned to the Movie camera symbol, so we'll start there. While using the M, Av, Tv, P, or B exposure modes while in that mode, five new menus are displayed. In Scene Intelligent Auto, Creative Auto, and Scene modes, there are just three options available.

Movie Shooting 1

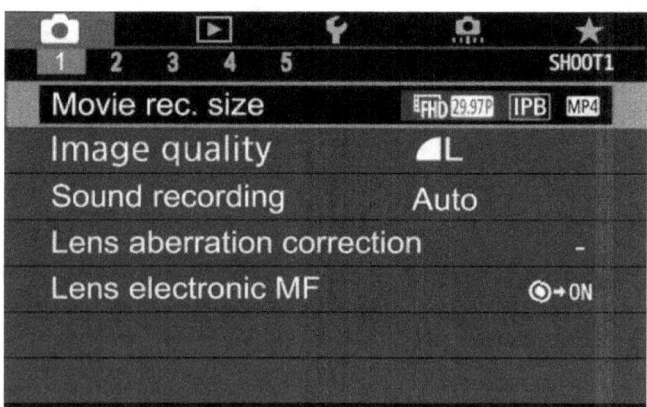

The Movie Shooting 1 menu has five settings.

- **Movie recording size:** Full HD video (1920 x 1080 pixels) can be recorded in 60/50, 30/25 (in both Standard and Light quality options), or 24 frames per second rates. Using either MOV or MP4 compression techniques, standard HD (1280 720 pixels) is available in 60/50 Standard quality and 30/25 Light quality.

- **Image Quality:** For still photos you take while in Movie mode, you can choose between RAW and JPEG standards here.

- **Sound Recording:** Choose Auto, Manual, or Disable; plus enable or disable wind filter and/or attenuation. In Basic Zone modes, your only choices are On or Off; when On is chosen, the recording level will be Auto, you cannot change the balance between left and right channels, and the wind filter (described shortly) will be automatically activated.

  → **Auto:** The 6D Mark II automatically selects the audio level for you.

  → **Manual:** There are 64 selectable sound levels. Choose Rec Level, turn the QCD, and keep an eye on the decibel meter at the bottom of the screen to choose a level that averages -12 dB for the loudest sounds.

  → **Disable:** Shot in silence, and then use your video editing program to add voiceover, narration, music, or other sound.

  Use the built-in microphones on your 6D Mark II, or attach a stereo microphone via the 3.5mm port on the side of the camera. The built-in microphone can easily pick up camera function, such as the autofocus motor in a lens, thus using an external microphone is a good idea.

→ **Wind attenuator/filter:** To lessen the effects of wind noise and the lowest bass tones, set Wind Filter to Auto. This lowers the low tones in the audio recording as well. If wind is not an issue, choosing Disable will result in higher-quality audio. Using an external microphone with a wind shield is an even better choice. Loud noises that aren't handled by the Auto or Manual sound recording settings are muted by the Attenuator feature.

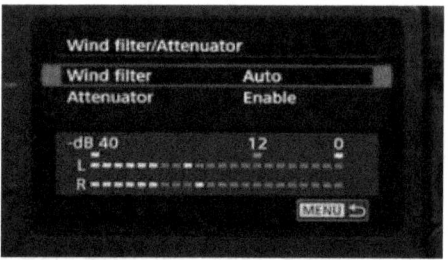

- **Lens aberration correction:** When utilizing movie mode, you can utilize two of the four adjustments, peripheral illumination correction and chromatic aberration correction.

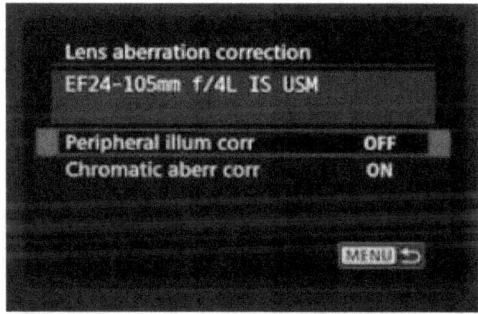

- Lens electronic MF.

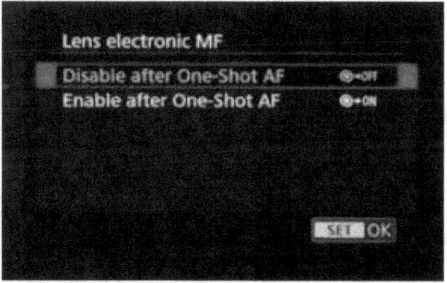

Movie Shooting 2

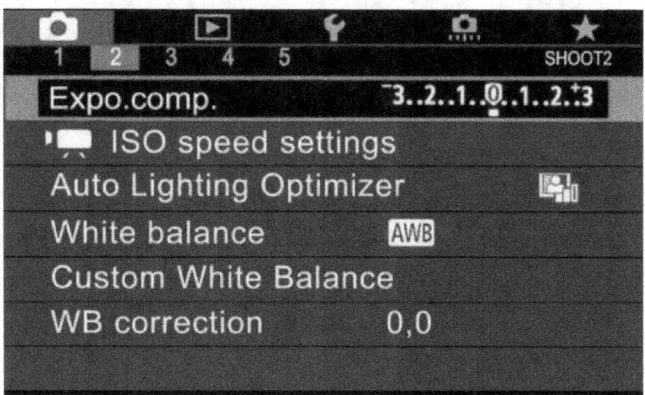

You'll find six entries in the Movie Shooting 2 menu.

- **Exposure compensation:** Operates similarly to still photography mode in video mode with the exception that bracketing cannot be performed.

- **Movie ISO speed settings:** Similar to the still-photo version, ISO settings cannot be manually selected, with the exception of when choosing Manual exposure. The 6D Mark II picks the appropriate ISO speed while using the P, Tv, Av, and B exposure modes. It should be noted that the L ISO setting is not used for video capturing (ISO 50 equivalent).

- **Speed Range:** The Minimum (100-12800) and Maximum ISO speeds are selectable (200–H2). If Highlight Tone Priority is turned on, the minimum and maximum values are 200 and 25600, respectively.

- **ISO Auto:** The highest ISO speed that will be chosen can only be ISO 6400-H2.

- **Time-lapse ISO Auto:** If you use the 6D Mark II's Time-Lapse mode, you can individually specify the highest ISO setting, which spans from ISO 400 to ISO 12600.

- **Auto Lighting Optimizer:** Working is the Auto Lighting Optimizer. It is not active while using manual or bulb exposure settings.

- **White balance:** Similar to how it would in still photography mode.

- **Custom white balance:** Functions similarly to still photography mode when using custom white balance.

- **White balance correction:** Correction for white balance: Functions the same as in still photography mode.

The Movie Shooting 3 menu only has three options. These are Highlight Tone Priority, High ISO Speed Noise Reduction, and Picture Style.

Movie Shooting 4

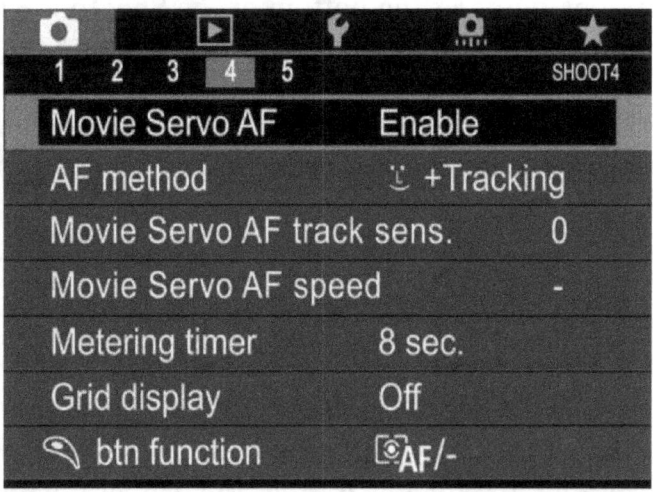

Seven entries make up the Movie Shooting 4 menu.

- **Movie Servo AF:** It is possible to enable or disable this feature, which allows the 6D Mark II to maintain focus on the subject when recording movies—even if the shutter button is not held down all the way. The constant refocusing could be inconvenient if the camera's built-in microphone picks up the noise and uses a lot of battery life. To momentarily turn off Cinema Servo AF, press the Flash button, the button you designated for that purpose using Custom Controls in the Custom Function 4 menu, or the Servo AF icon in the LCD monitor's bottom left corner. Once video shooting has been restarted and the MENU or Playback button has been pushed, or after switching the AF technique. video Servo AF will automatically continue. If Movie Servo has been disabled, press the shutter button or the AF-ON button halfway to begin focusing. You can modify the Movie Servo AF speed and tracking sensitivity using two options found at the bottom of the Shooting 4 (Movie) menu.

- **AF Method:** Face Detection+Tracking, Smooth Zone, and Live 1 Point AF are the same AF modes that are accessible in live view.

- **Movie Servo AF Track Sensitivity:** The next entry and entry are only accessible if Live 1 Point AF (above) is enabled. for the 6D Mark II, ranging from Locked On (-3 to -1) to Responsive (+1 to +3), gives you the option to select from one of five tracking sensitivity settings. Use this parameter to tell the camera whether to immediately begin tracking a new topic or to remain focused on the present one.

- **Servo AF speed for movies:** This entry is only accessible if Live 1 Point AF is enabled. You can specify an AF Speed that ranges from fast (+2) to regular (0) to slow, as well as whether Movie Servo AF is active always or only while the camera is being used to take pictures (saving battery life) (–7). For example, STM motor-equipped lenses allow incremental focus shifts for more fluid refocusing throughout a photo.

- **Metering Timer:** Tell us how long the metering system will be active before it shuts down. In addition to 4, 16, or 30 seconds, you have a choice of 1, 10, or 30 minutes. Tap the shutter release to restart the timer.

- **Grid Display:** The same choices as those listed under Live View settings are available.

- **Shutter button function:** Allows for the alteration of the shutter button's functions when moving pictures are being taken. The optional Remote Switch RS-80N3, Timer Remote Controller TC80N3, and Wireless Remote Control BR-E1 can also be used to start/stop movie capture. Please note that any settings you have established for the shutter button using C.Fn III-4 Custom Controls for still photography are superseded by these parameters when the camera is in video mode.

Movie Shooting 5

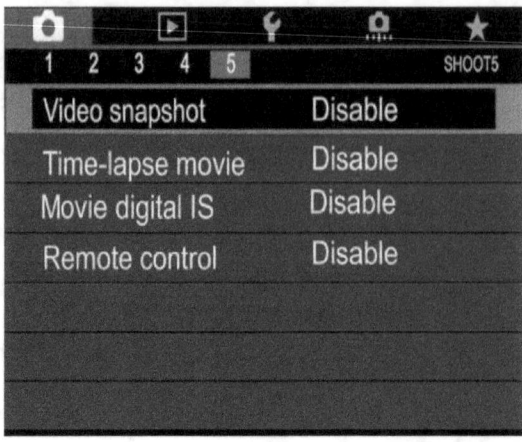

There are four entries in the Movie Shooting 5 menu.

- **Video Snapshot:** Enables/disables video snapshots.

- **Time-lapse movie:** Enables/disables time-lapse movies.

- **Movie Digital IS:** Enables/disables electronic image stabilization, which I'll explain next.

- **Remote control:** Enables starting or stopping movie capture using the optional Remote Controller RC-6, and Wireless Remote Control BR-E1.

Exposure Options

You have the option of using totally automatic exposure while shooting videos, choosing to specify exposure in Manual exposure mode, or selecting a shutter speed or aperture setting that you like for artistic reasons. With the exception of Manual exposure mode, the 6D Mark II will automatically choose an

ISO speed for you. The AF point selection button is to the right of the * button, and it can be used to unlock exposure and unlock it again. Following are your choices:

- **Fully automatic exposure:** The 6D Mark II will select the best exposure for you if the Mode Dial is set to Basic Zone modes, such as Scene Intelligent Auto or Scene modes. Even if the Mode Dial is set to Tv (Shutter-priority), Av (Aperture-priority), or B, the exposure will be configured as if you had selected P. (Bulb exposure). Be cautious that switching to the B position will prevent the camera from taking a bulb or time exposure and instead cause it to go to P. The objective is to prevent you from accidentally choosing B and disabling video recording.

- **Exposure Compensation:** When using Creative Zone modes, flip the Lock switch to the down position. Then, you can adjust exposure compensation by rotating the Quick Control Dial.

- **Speedlite movie light:** If you have a Canon Speedlite with an integrated movie LED light mounted and turned on (such the Speedlite 320EX), the 6D Mark II will automatically turn the lamp on in low light situations when you are using exposure modes other than M (Manual).

- **Manual exposure:** Choose M on the Mode Dial and you can specify ISO speed, shutter speed, and aperture.

    → **ISO:** To display the ISO speed setting screen, press the ISO Compensation button on top of the camera. Use the Main Dial to adjust. Selecting Auto will cause the camera to choose the proper ISO based on the shutter speed and aperture you have chosen. If you chose Auto, the * button during Manual exposure locks the ISO at the current level.

→ **Shutter speed:** Under the restrictions outlined under Shutter-priority AE earlier, choose a shutter speed using the Main Dial.

→ **Aperture:** Aperture adjustment is done via the Quick Control Dial.

Formats, Compression, Resolution, and Frame Rates

Even intermediate movie shooters can be confused by the number of different choices for format, compression, resolution, and frame rates. This section will help clarify things for you by explaining what each of these terms means, and what options are available to you.

MP4 Formats/Compression

The 6D Mark II uses the industry-standard MP4 format for video. The popular Mac format MOV isn't supported, however, most video editors can convert your MP4 files into MOV if both were created using the same codec (video encoder, such as H.264). The MP4 formats' real compression techniques are simple to comprehend. The 6D Mark II stores files utilizing IPB

(I-frame/P-frame/B-frame) Standard and Light and the common H.264/MPEG-4 codec ("coder-decoder").

IPB is a compression technique applied to MP4 files. It uses interframe compression, which means that just a select few "key" frames are retained, while the remaining frames are "simulated" or extrapolated from the data in the frames that come before and after them. P-frames are "predicted picture" frames that only capture pixel changes from the previous frame (for example, a runner moving across a fixed background); B-frames are "bi-predictive picture" frames that combine the differences from the previous and following frames. I-frames are the entire frames or intraframes. This interpolation results in files with smaller sizes but slightly inferior image quality, which uses more of your camera's DIGIC 7 processing power.

IPB-encoded video needs to be transcoded into a format that can be edited with your video-editing program. Particularly in frames with a lot of motion occurring throughout the frame, the compression strategy may result in more artifacts. I only employ this technique when being able to shoot farther is crucial. The 6D Mark II offers two versions: Standard, which simultaneously compresses multiple frames for improved efficiency and smaller file sizes; and Light, which records at a slower bit rate than Standard but still produces smaller files and is more compatible with a wider range of playback systems.

Each movie clip has a maximum runtime of 29 minutes and 59 seconds, and SD/SDHC memory cards (those with 32GB or less capacity) have a maximum file size of 4GB.

Here is a listing of some of the limitations you'll run up against:

- **4GB Limit with SD/SDHC cards:** If your memory card is bigger than 4GB when you start recording a video and the file size surpasses 4GB, you can keep recording. The elapsed shooting time shown on the LCD will start blinking about 30 seconds before the 4GB file size is reached. A new movie file will be generated automatically if you go past 4GB. This procedure is repeated up until the 29 minutes, 59 second maximum shooting time. You'll need to use a movie-editing application to join them or play each movie file separately. You can record clips bigger than 4GB on SDXC memory cards (those bigger than 32GB); the movie will be recorded as a single file. However, after the 29:59 time limit is met (explained later), the camera will stop recording. It should be noted that video files greater than 4GB cannot be transferred using other methods, including the wireless capabilities of the 6D Mark II, and must be transferred to your computer using the EOS Utility or a memory card reader.

- **29:59 Limit:** This restriction was allegedly put in place because equipment that can record for more than 30 minutes is subject to a higher tax rate when classified as "camcorders" in some jurisdictions. Movie capture stops after the allotted shooting time is up and does not resume itself. To begin a new movie file, you must press the Start/Stop button once more.

- **MP4 Format:** Full HD; IPB compression allows you to record in MP4 format for 8 to 17 minutes before hitting the 4GB cap, however IPB Light only allows you to record for 29:59.

- **MP4 Format:** Standard HD; Using IPB Standard and IPB Light, you can record for 20 to 29:59 minutes, respectively. When filming HDR videos, the 4GB limit will be reached after roughly 17 minutes.

Resolution/Movie Recording Size

Resolution (Movie Recording Size) choices are a little less techie:

- **1920 × 1080 (1080p):** The highest resolution that can be seen while using the HDTV format is called "Full HD" by Canon. (The higher quality 4K format is inaccessible to the 6D Mark II.) You can select this resolution to get the best image quality on most HD televisions and most monitors. Use this resolution for your "professional" projects, particularly if you plan to edit and create attractive DVDs from them. The highest resolution, however, uses the most storage capacity. Using the option in the Movie Shooting 1 menu, choose Movie Recording Quality. A quick Class 10 card is advised since Full HD requires transfer rates of 216-431 MB/min to write to your memory card, depending on your frame rate.

- **1280 × 720 (720p):** The term "HD" is used by Canon, while "Standard HD" or "SHD" is more frequently used. It offers lower quality and may be viewed on any monitor or HDTV-compatible television. This resolution is suitable if your production will only be viewed on

81

HDTVs with a 720p maximum resolution or computer monitors with a resolution of 1280 720. With IPB compression, this resolution uses a transfer rate of 184 MB/min at 60/50 frames per second, thus it won't necessarily put a strain on your memory cards.

- **HDR movie shooting:** When the Mode Dial is set to Scene mode, this option is automatically used. Either IPB (Standard) or IPB (Light) quality options let you select 60/50 frames per second. Dynamic range is improved by HDR video by enhancing highlight details in bright sections of an image.

Frame rates

Frame rates are simple to select in the 6D Mark II world, because all video is shot using progressive scan and interlaced scan is not a choice. (With progressive scan, all the lines in a frame are collected consecutively; interlacing captures even and odd numbered lines of each frame alternately.) Fortunately, one seemingly complex set of options may be simply eliminated: You can think of the 50/25 fps and 60/30 fps options as complementary pairings of frame rates for videos. Only regions with the NTSC television standard in place—including North America, Japan, Korea, Mexico, and a few other places—use the 60/30 fps rates. Where the PAL standard is in use, such as in Europe, Russia, China, Africa, Australia, and other regions, the 50/25 frame rates are employed. I'll only use the 60/30 frame rate in this section for the sake of simplicity; if you're reading this in India, just convert to 50/25.

The third option is 24 frames per second (fps), which is the usual frame rate for movies. The charges are minimal, so keep that in mind. In reality, 24 frames per second produces 23.976 frames, and 30 frames per second produces 29.97 actual "frames" each second.

The distinction can be found between the two "worlds" of motion pictures, film and video. The frame rate for motion picture film is typically 24 fps, while video is typically 30 fps, at least in the NTSC-using countries of the United States, Japan, and other places. Both types can be handled and converted by computer editing tools. What you intend to do with your video will determine whether you choose 24 or 30 frames per second.

The gist of it is that 24 frames per second provides your video a "film" look, which is great for displaying fine detail. However, 24 fps can result in a jerky effect known as "judder" if your clip contains moving subjects or you pan the camera. While some consider the image of a 30 or 60 fps rate to be less appealing, it is smoother and less jerky when viewed on an electronic monitor. I advise you to experiment with both and select the frame rate and video-editing program that best suit your preferences.

Quick Control

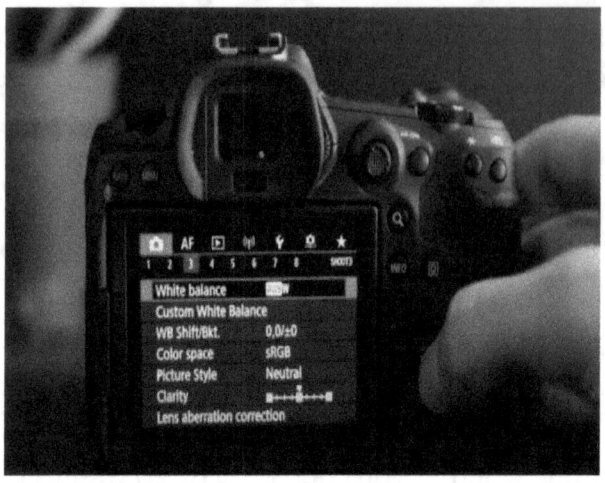

You may reach a Quick Control screen by pressing the Q button, much like when taking still photos. You can set the parameters for Video Snapshot as well as the AF Method, Movie Recording Size, Movie Digital Image Stabilization, White Balance, Picture Style, and Auto Lighting Optimizer in Creative Zone modes. Only when Manual adjustment has been selected is it possible to change the sound level.

Video Snapshots

Video snapshots are collections of identically sized movie segments that play as a single film. For all of the clips in a certain album, you can specify a constant length of 2, 4, or 8 seconds. I use the 2-second length to create mini-movies of rapidly occurring events, like parades, giving me a dynamic collection of clips that capture everything happening without spending too much time on any one scene. Landscapes and many travel-related clips are perfect for the 8-second timeframe since the longer sceneries offer you time to take in all the intriguing things to observe in such locations. The 4-second clips are a great method to highlight specifics of a single subject, such as the architecture of a cathedral or other landmark while touring, or to provide a quick rundown of the action at a sporting event.

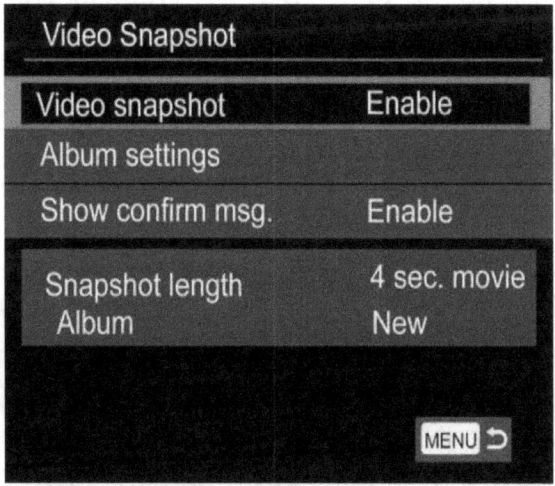

First, turn on the Movie Shooting 5 menu's video snapshot option:

1. **Activate:** The Movie Shooting 5 menu, and then choose Video Snapshot.

2. **Enable snapshots:** Draw attention to the Video Snapshot entry, hit SET, choose Enable, and then press SET once again for confirmation.

3. **Select album:** Next, select Create a New Album or Add to Existing Album from the Album Settings menu.

4. **Indicate the Snapshot Length:** A popup with the statement "The next video snapshot will be added to a new album" and the option to select Snapshot Length appears if you select Create a New Album. Choose 2 Sec. Movie, 4 Sec. Movie, or 8 Sec. Movie after selecting that option and pressing SET. To confirm your selection, press SET.

5. **Verify the settings:** Returning to the previous screen is what happens. If OK is highlighted, press SET or tap OK.

6. **Enable/Disable Confirm Msg:** When it is turned on, a message on the screen will invite you to Add to Album, Save As a New Album, Playback Video Snapshot, or Delete Without Saving to Album. If you choose Disable, the camera skips this process, saves your video snapshot automatically, and is then prepared to take another picture. If you intended to take multiple video captures one after another without having to reply to the confirmation message each time, you should disable the confirmation message.

7. **Exit:** To finish setting up Video Snapshot, press/tap MENU. You may get a more thorough explanation on how to use the feature in the next section.

Conventional movie shooting is disabled while Video Snapshot is enabled. Instead, the 6D Mark II records a clip of the chosen duration each time you push the Start/Stop button. Following are the steps in the process:

1. **Take a snapshot of the video:** Press the Start/Stop button while in movie mode. A blue bar will appear as soon as the 6D Mark II starts recording a clip, indicating how much time is left before recording automatically ends.

2. **Save your clip as a collection of video snapshots:** The film will be saved to the current album if the confirmation message has been deactivated. where you can take another picture. The confirmation message is displayed overlaid on the Playback screen that you've chosen by pressing the INFO. button.

3. **Pick the option for confirmation:** Depending on whether this is the first clip for an album or another clip, you can use the left/right multi-controller directional buttons or the touch screen to choose Save As Album/Add To Album, Save to New Album, Playback Video Snapshot (that you just took), or Do Not Save to Album/Delete Without Saving to Album (exit without adding to an album).

4. **Click SET:** Your very first clip will serve as the album's debut.

5. **Capture more videos:** To capture additional clips of the length you've selected, as shown by the blue bars at the bottom of the frame, press the Movie button. The confirmation screen will reappear at the conclusion of the allotted time.

6. **Add to the album or make a new one:** If you want to add the most recent clip to the album you just started, select the leftmost icon once more. As an alternative, you can select the Save as a New Album icon, which is the second icon from the left, by pressing the left/right multi-controller directional buttons. Your previous album will be finished as a result, and a new one will begin with the most recent clip.

   Choose the Playback Video Snapshot icon (second from the right) to review the most recent clip you shot if you want to make sure it's worth adding to an album. The options after that are to delete the clip or add it to an album.

7. **Remove recent clip:** You can choose Do Not Save to Album/Delete without Saving to Album (the rightmost icon) if you decide the most recent clip is not one you want to include in your current album.

8. **Change from traditional movie clips to video snapshots:** If you want to stop shooting video snapshots and resume shooting conventional movie clips (of a customizable duration), navigate to the Movie Shooting 5 menu again, and disable Video Snapshot.

Note: Once you've set up the Video Snapshot feature, you can rapidly enable or stop it using the Quick Control menu. The Video Snapshot symbol is the bottom icon in the left row of the Quick Control menu.

www.ingramcontent.com/pod-product-compliance
Lightning Source LLC
Chambersburg PA
CBHW070439220526
45466CB00004B/1736